A Brief History of
Two Aprons

poems by

Merna Dyer Skinner

Finishing Line Press
Georgetown, Kentucky

A Brief History of Two Aprons

ACKNOWLEDGMENTS

I am grateful to the following journals for publishing these poems:

Mojave River Review, "A Brief History of Two Aprons" and "Catch and Release" (in
an earlier version).
MiPOesias, "How To Talk Your Way Out of a Traffic Ticket in a Foreign Country"
Squaw Valley Review and *Silver Birch Press,* (as part of their "Me As a Child" series),
"Southern Bound White Girl"
Star 82 Review, "Before Gravity"

Thank you to my teachers and mentors from UCLA Writers Extension Program,
Writing Workshops Los Angeles, Tupelo Press Workshops and the Squaw Valley
Community of Writers: Rick Bursky, Elline Lipkin, Edan Lapucki, Lou Matthews,
Barbara Abercrombie, Jeffrey Levine, Mark Doty, Robert Hass, CD Wright and
Matthew Zapruder.

My great appreciation to my first reader, Phyllis Behar, and to my many writers
group members, especially the Ninjas. And, to Terry Lucas who is not only a caring
reader with a keen ear and eye, but also an enviable poet — and proof that a casual
conversation can lead to great things.

Finally, thank you to Finishing Line Press editors Leah Maines and Christen Kincaid
for their support and care in bringing my first collection of poems to life.

Editor: Christen Kincaid

Cover Art: "Letting Go," painting by Margie Mirell,
mirellpsychotherapy.com

Author Photo: Courtesy of Mark Bennington Photography,
www.markbenningphotography.com

Cover Design: Elizabeth Maines

Table of Contents

For my mother, Raye

for my grandmothers, Iva Leona and Clara Louise

and

for Sean and Drew, always

Oh, to possess the strength of a gladiola stem!
The vast distance from its base to its tip
where heavy blossoms hang,
yet the stem never bends.

—Gladioli in a Clear Vase
(At the Feet of a Poet Reading)

A BRIEF HISTORY OF TWO APRONS

She hangs the gingham apron loose around her neck. Frayed grosgrain ribbons edge three pockets. Sewn in her youth and stored in her hope chest, the apron hangs low over breasts heavy as breadfruit. She pulls wooden clothespins from a pocket. Bites them between her teeth. It is laundry day on the prairie. She hangs her man's clothes — lets them stiffen on the line. An errant rooster feather clings to his shirt snapping in the wind. She plucks it off and tucks the bit of red in her pocket. She will tickle him with it later.

She pulls the butcher's apron over her head. Wraps the ties twice around her waist. Her white sheath catches drips of red as she lifts a tray of beef scraps. It is hamburger-grinding day. She pushes twenty pounds of cow through churning metal teeth, blends it into strings of red meat. Smeared with blood by the end of her shift, she flicks errant bits of gristle from her chest, wipes the knives clean against her white thighs. She will cash her check at the corner bar — lick white foam from atop a stream of beers and kiss any man with clean nails.

CATCH AND RELEASE

Father's thick fingers bait our hooks and cast our lines,
sending shimmying circles across the lake. When
the ripples smooth to nothing, I sigh, as if with them. I am five.

Dragonflies helicopter overhead. My line jerks with my first fish —
too small to keep. Father releases it — it's mother-of-pearl scales
    glimmering in the
morning light, cold body undulating deeper until it disappears.

Shrimp carapace scattered on a white plate. I am twenty-five.
The difference between the wind in my hair and the wind on the waves —
nothing more than quarks in motion here or there.

Buttery fingers wiped on white linen leave the DNA
of ancient crustaceans. On the table, a splayed lobster tail,
crab shells sucked dry and the diamond ring I've cast aside.

I slip from the room while this man who once seemed so alluring
takes a call. Survival is a question of instinct, moving this way
rather than that. Seeing the bait bag for what it is — a test.

Where Do You Feel Most At Home?

How to describe the sound of a turning page?
A crinkle, a caress, a luffing sail?
Paper brushes page, emitting a swish, so exotic
I envision myself a goddess strolling the Kasbah.
My fine gown's finger-laced train glides over Moroccan tiles
like a whisper.

How to describe the features of a fine volume?
Leather bound, creamy aged vellum —
feathered edges, raw, tint of vermillion
as if a knick-edged ax had cleaved each sheet from redwoods.
Or the pliant leather cover of my grandfather's book —
sacred-skinned pages, translucent in the sunlight —
heavy with words that have sent men to war.
In the margins, grandfather's notes — Indian ink echoes
of his century-old Sunday morning sermons.

Outside my window, a thwack on the porch beckons me
to *The New York Times* and hot jasmine tea.
Messy, noisy newsprint smudges my fingers —
like the purple-thumbed testimony of Middle Eastern voters
my ink stains declare: *I am a reader.*

In my library, small as a womb, I linger —
swaddled in stillness — interrupted
only by the music of pages
played by my thumb and fingers.

CONNECTING THREADS

My grandmother, a penny square,
my mother cut from whole cloth —
and I, a mystery quilt.

Who's fingers cross-stitched my
muslin skin? Who over-stuffed
my trapunto thighs?

My spirit, bias cut, still strains
against gender-rigid seams
stitched in the 1950's.

My aging, raw edges need rebinding
lest I unravel into a maze
of tangled threads.

My hips, like fat quarter,
need strip piecing.
Lower the feed dogs,

mend my tears —
with gentle hands,
camouflage my scars
with golden thread.

1949

The year I am Michigan born — wispy blonde and pink as albino bunny eyes. Further east, Paul Robeson's color tops headlines as Peekskill citizens lynch the singer in effigy.

A man can't sing once his throat's throttled, even if only symbolically.

In other black and white news, Polaroid sells its first boxy Land Camera, producing black & white photos in one minute. The impatient pay $89.95.

American medium income: $2,600 — minus 3% if you buy the camera.

Unemployment peaks at 7.9% and Arthur Miller's *Death of a Salesman* comes to Broadway. *The NY Times* heralds it as "heroic, a suburban epic."

My father opens his first grocery store. Sells everything from apples to azaleas.

In Texas, Capt. Gallagher lands Lucky Lady II, completing the first round-the-world nonstop flight. In Asia, the state of Vietnam forms, perhaps as Lucky Lady flies overhead.

Many baby boys gurgling beside me in the hospital nursery will die in Vietnam.

While RCA perfects color broadcasting, every pro-basketball player in the newly formed NBA is white. It will be the last league to integrate.

The NFL led the way in '46, baseball in '47.

In Ecuador, six thousand die in a major earthquake. In the US, six million more babies are born — even with black mothers and babies dying at twice the rate of whites.

At 21 inches, I join what Sylvia Porter will call the 'baby boom" generation.

In Russia, "reds" test "First Lightening," their first atomic bomb. The U.S. convicts eleven Communist leaders of plotting violent insurrections. Cold War is on the march.

My father refuses to build a bomb shelter. When I am six, I will practice "Duck-and-Cover" drills at Northwestern Elementary.

The year I am born, President Truman pulls troops from Korea, recognizes the state of Israel and sends millions in aid to Palestinian refugees.

Expanding land that occupies the same space is still impossible.

On June 30, 1949 — Dutch troops evacuate Djakarta. In Michigan, forceps pull me from my mother's womb.

Two days later, my mother goes dancing at the Lake Lansing Inn. Vaughn Monroe sings *Riders In the Sky*. I'm left in a dresser drawer, baby bottle propped on a pillow.

— it's true, I have the Polaroid to prove it —

MY PARIS BIRTHDAY

In the early morning, mother and I stroll the Catacombs.
Empty skulls stacked fifty deep. In each,
five dark openings to take life in, let breath out.
A beetle crawls through a bullet hole.

In the Picasso Museum, Carlos Casagemas,
captive of Picasso's canvas, longs
to cover the gunshot wound to his temple.
His blood flows forever for all to see.

The beginning of his Blue Period says the docent.
Testimony to my Love's rejection mumbles Carlos.
At the Opera House, Salome kisses the lips
of the saint's severed head plated for her pleasure.
Music of her savage desire scored by Strauss.

Where is my cake? Where is my celebration?
In Place Dauphine, a lone bird defecates on my yellow hair.
My mother, whose blood runs black with disease,
toasts my good fortune. On the day of my birth,
in the city of lights, I see only death,
my dying mother, only luminance.

HOW TO TALK YOUR WAY OUT OF A TRAFFIC TICKET IN A FOREIGN COUNTRY

And Officer, it was as if the tree reached out from the woods,
just there — do you see the slick of leaves and snapped branches?
And the rain beat down so hard the wipers wept

and my eyes stung with smoky mascara. Sir,
the mascara — it's not supposed to run. Why does everything run?

And that pine fence blew loose, blocking my path.
And the funeral, it's started by now, and I'm not there, sir.

Lo siento, sir. It's getting cold. You have snow on your mustache,
sir. Yes, so easy to brush away — still, snow can smother a boy.
Lo siento, sir. My papers must be here, buried in my bag.

Do you have children, sir? Niños? You're lucky. Perhaps
it was the mailbox I passed — with its latch undone. And I was
*   wondering,*
will the casket be open? Do they do that here? I was wondering,
will my son's blue eyes still shimmer beneath his brittle lids?

SOUTHERN BOUND WHITE GIRL

Traveling slow as heat along the Dixie Highway
we pass bare bottom brown boys digging in dirt.
An old woman sits outside her one-room shack
fanning her skin, creased as dried mud.

Further on, a khaki-covered white man
sits atop a horse — rifle in hand.
Bound ankles shuffle, chains clink a dusty song
and twenty sweat-soaked black backs
bend, digging a ditch already dug. Across the field
a bright Georgia road sign promises
  Peaches Grits Biscuits Just Ahead

  ―――――――――

  White Only   Colored
I am six — sunburned pink
I follow the arrow for Colored

SKINLESS GIRL

The girl crawled out of her skin and kicked it to the corner. *I'm feeling ugly today,* she said to the dust bunnies gathering under the bed. They felt pretty and light and so said nothing.

The girl was certain her troubles began the day her first pimple appeared. She awoke that humid morning to the pulsing of a second heartbeat — coming from the nape of her neck. In the mirror she saw the red, throbbing pustule, pumping puss, pulsing and pushing against her skin. All summer that protrusion grew and grew until the girl could no longer hold up her head.

BEFORE GRAVITY

Remember when we skipped everywhere?
Arms moving like counterpoint melodies,
knees rising, pedaling air,
ponytails swinging, whipping our backs,
slapping our faces.
Bouncing along concrete squares
cautious to never land on a crack
(even on days we cared little for mother).
Skipping swiftly, our bodies lifting from earth,
repeating that singular sensation, that beat of a second
when we were suspended in space —
no longer rising, not yet falling.
So light, so light.

AN UNDISCIPLINED ODE TO A RESCUE DOG

You came at me like a bullet —
all broad nose and wild, wide-set eyes.
My arm hairs prickled as you shot towards me —
black fur, rippling mass of muscle, paws the size of mugs.
Pit Bull.

Abandoned in the woods of West Virginia —
your crooked tail bent at 90 degrees — probably kinked
by a car door. Ears severely clipped, like Batman points
atop your boxy brow.
Mad dog.

But you were smart.
Learned that I was your pack leader.
Learned that other dogs weren't squirrels to chase.
Learned three languages: s'asseoir, hinsetzen, sit, Zoë!
Bon chien.

In gift shops, no crocheted pillows of pit bulls, no cups, no caps
no Christmas ornaments. Good manners got you nowhere —
people crossed the street when you approached. No
one patted your head.
Unmarketable dog.

To others you were a thug, a biker-chick, to me, a marshmallow
coated in fur. We crossed the country together, left
New York for LA — me, your Steinbeck — you my Charley,
your head resting on my arm as I drove.
Buddy dog.

In Venice, we found our packs — Muscle Beach dog and poet.
You ran in the sand, sun so bright we didn't see the cancer
until your legs collapsed and your bullet speed stopped.
— then your breath, then my heart.
Gone dog.

PULLING UP ROOTS

I come from fresh water lakes and salt-water taffy,
From chrome-bumpered cars with custom made chassis,

I come from clean highway rest stops, inner-city chop shops,
From fruit stands and fresh pies with finger-pinched crusts on top,

I come from skinned knees on splintery docks, from Big Ten football
    jocks,
From cheerleading squads, hot rod cars and *SUNDAY! SUNDAY!* at the
    track.

I come from white sheets on clotheslines and mongrel dogs on chains,
From canasta playing grandmothers serving fresh lemonade,

I come from women who tend gardens and men who hunt deer,
From pine-bough-slapping sweat lodges where they beat your skin clear,

I come from colonizers, proselytizers, a religious martyr (she did swing)
From shoemakers, Great Lakers, a pilot, some farmers, a king.

But, who cares where I've come from?
— it's where I'm going — it's what *I* bring.

J'ACCUSE CHARTREUSE

Chartreuse, you're a ruse, with a capital R.
Your name confuses me — sounding
other than what you really are.

Chartreuse, the very word
conjures crimson in my mind —
a smoky stage, a raspy chanteuse

singing of love in blood-red shoes.
In truth, chartreuse, you are tertiary,
half way between two hues —

an innocent yellow that slept
with a wandering green
and gave birth to your neon sheen.

I'd like to think, chartreuse,
that inside your lemony yellow
and crickety green

there beats a predilection,
a throbbing Redness
that is the true you —
                    cha-R-treuse

A PRIVATE REVEILLE

The cook slips from the kitchen
in the pre-dawn grey,
wipes his hands along his apron,
crosses the gravel drive.

Like a soldier, he pivots,
snapping to attention—unaware
of me on the balcony above—
my morning meditation interrupted.

Still and straight as a fence stake,
he faces the Truchas Peaks.
His chest rises and falls once
before the sun spills over
the New Mexican range,
lights his face and hair.

With a nod, he turns crisply,
crunches back across the stones,
disappears into the kitchen
where he will crack eggs
and chop potatoes for
a lodge of still sleeping strangers.

WITHOUT WARNING

When you last
climbed
into my bed
did you know
it was the last?
Did you know
you would
leave
a burnished
imprint
of your body
on my sheets
that I cannot
remove?
Or is it
my body
I see
lying there
like a corpse
shadow
on a sidewalk
in Hiroshima?

MISTAKES

I keep a can of Gesso
near me as I write.
I do not want
to delete the first words
that step forward.
I want to lay down
layers of language —
thought threads
that may tear or fray.
The words composed
on this page are only
the first.

MISTAKES

I keep a can of Gesso
near me as I write.
I do not want
to delete words
that surface first.
I want to spread
layers of language —
thought threads
that rip and tear.
The words composed
on this page conceal
ones you should not see.

MISTAKES

I keep a can of Gesso
near me as I write.
I do not want
to erase the words
that surface first.
I want to build
layers of language —
bind the thought threads
that otherwise fray and tear.
The words on this page
long to last.

THEIR WEIGHT IS IN THEIR WEIGHTLESSNESS
from Yannis Ritsos' Bitter Knowledge

Where does a thing go when it burns?

Still as stone, I stare at charred bits
of grandmother's house. My six-year old mind
conjures a sinister magician
spinning his red cloak over her home,
choking her awake with a whoosh
of black smoke.
His flame-throwing wand scorches her roof.
He lifts his cape — and voila!

    The box of her life disappears.

I shuffle through the soot of burnt books,
umber-edged photos, skeins of yarn,
her shawl fused to the sofa.
My patent leather shoes lose their gloss
as ashes, delicate as moths' wings,
rise and flutter in my wake.
Near the front stone steps that lead to nothing
but sky, I lift a lilac blossom from the singed bush
and inhale

    all that remains.

I WASN'T ALWAYS BROKEN

She unzips my wrist
Slips tendons aside
Reconnects bits of bone.

       In Qin Shi Huang
       Eight thousand terra cotta soldiers
       Sun baked from earth's mud
       Stand guard, hollow bodies whole.

Rain-soaked grass, rootless as a toupee,
Lies loose atop a Santa Monica hillside
Fools my trusting step, fractures my frame.

Fifteen sutures
Single file over seven screws
One metal plate
Two plaster casts.

       Clay horses and chariots stand
       Intact for two thousand years
       Ready, fixed.

A watery snare, exposed
In a circle of streetlight last night.
A leaky hose, a gathering pool —
Repairs, temporary — solidity an illusion.

ROW AND REST

Lift the oar
From the water
Let it rest across
The bow

Rivulets trickle
To the oar's lip
Drip and drop
Slither and slip

Back to mother lake
Like children
sidling home

Merna Dyer Skinner is a poet, photographer, and essayist, and has worked as a business communications consultant for three decades. She is the President and Founder of Satori Communications, Inc.

While her writing often reflects her Midwest Michigan roots, Merna has lived in Boston, New York, Miami and Los Angeles, and has traveled to four of the seven continents. Her travel photography has been shown in numerous New York locations.

She graduated Magna Cum Laude from Emerson College with a Masters Degree in Communication Studies. As an undergraduate, Merna attended Michigan State University before transferring to the University of West Florida where she graduated with honors, earning two Bachelor of Arts Degrees in English and Communication Arts.

Her business articles have appeared in national publications including: *The Wall Street Journal, Investor's Business Daily* and *The Pfeiffer Book of Successful Communication Skill-Building Tools.* She has prepared authors and executives for national broadcast media interviews on *The Today Show, The Charlie Rose Show,* and *NPR,* among others.

Her poetry has been published in both print and online literary journals including: *MiPOesias, Star 82 Review, Mojave River Review, Silver Birch Press* and *Squaw Valley Review.* She is an alumna of the Squaw Valley Writers Community, UCLA Writers Extension Program, Writing Workshops Los Angeles and Tupelo Press Poetry Workshop.

Merna is the mother of two sons, Sean and Drew, and shares her Venice, California home with Sophie, her sixth rescue dog, a Golden Retriever rescued from Taiwan.

For more information, please visit her website at:
www.mernadyerskinner.com